$17.99 US / $25.99 CAN hardcover
$15.99 US / $23.99 CAN softcover

Let the island breezes of Realla (pronounced Ree all ya!) settle you into front row seats among the butterflies, mongooses and Metronoma city workers, as they enjoy the musical stylings of the Notable Characters. These five kids make it a routine to play music in Poplar Park every midday break from school, but they are confronted with a misguided, sometimes mean-spirited group of sisters and their little brother Un Rest, who feel slighted by the Notables because of all the attention they are getting with their songs. Come and enjoy this story while getting an introduction to basic features of reading, writing and performing music.

The Notable Characters
© 2017 by Leonard B. Rountree.
℗ 2017 by Washen Publishing, a division of Washentertainment.
All rights reserved.

Copyright © 2017 by Leonard B. Rountree. All rights reserved.
Printed and distributed in the United States of America.
Published ℗ 2017 by Washen Publishing, a division of Washentertainment
ISBN: 978-0-692-92202-6

Audio recordings of the following songs related to the Notable Characters story are:
* "We Had Our Nap We Had Our Meal and Now We Feel Okay"
* "Noise Will Be Noise"
* "Doing the Rest Stop"
* "Swirl"

Also featured in the musical production of Swirl, based on "The Notable Characters"

The latter three songs are heard on the album "Gainful Enjoyment"
All songs written, arranged, produced, and recorded at the Washen Machine Studio in Cheverly, Maryland U.S.A.
Copyright © 2017 By Leonard B. Rountree a.k.a. Lenny Rountree

Audio book version is narrated by the author.
Voice characterizations are performed by Lenny Rountree and Rachael L. Byrd

No part of this book, be it audio, visual, characterizations or text may be reproduced or transmitted in any form or by any means, electronic or mechanical, including photocopying, recording or by any information storage and retrieval system, without express written permission from the publisher, except in the case of brief quotations embodied in critical reviews and articles.

Dedicated to my mother Joyce Marie Howard and my father Lawrence Rountree
who encouraged me to pursue writing and music as a career.
– Lenny Rountree

A Quick Note from the Author:

Notes are visual symbols for sounding sounds, and rests are visual symbols for taking short breaks from making sounds altogether. As you read this book, notice how the Notes and Rests appear in the story. Enjoy!

In the seaside city of Metronoma on the hilly Caribbean island of Realla (pronounced re-all-ya), there live five Kiddy-o's called Notable Characters. They all share a love of sound, such as the sound of mongoose scurrying along pebbles and grass in Poplar Park, the sound of seagulls performing their roll call on the sandy beaches, and especially the sound of musical instruments.

Wholesome is the oldest of the Notable Characters and he sets a good example for the others to follow. His three eyes suit him well for playing drums and percussion. These instruments require coordination and sensitivity. Wholesome possesses both.

Percussion instruments include timbales, congas, bongos, cajons, guiras, and djembe drums. He keeps a steady beat and leads the younger Characters safely from their homes on Tone Row across the street to Poplar Park.

Dutch plays the double bass and the electric bass. Both instruments have four thickly wound strings which stretch across a narrow wooden neck. These strings vibrate when you move them with your fingers or a pick.

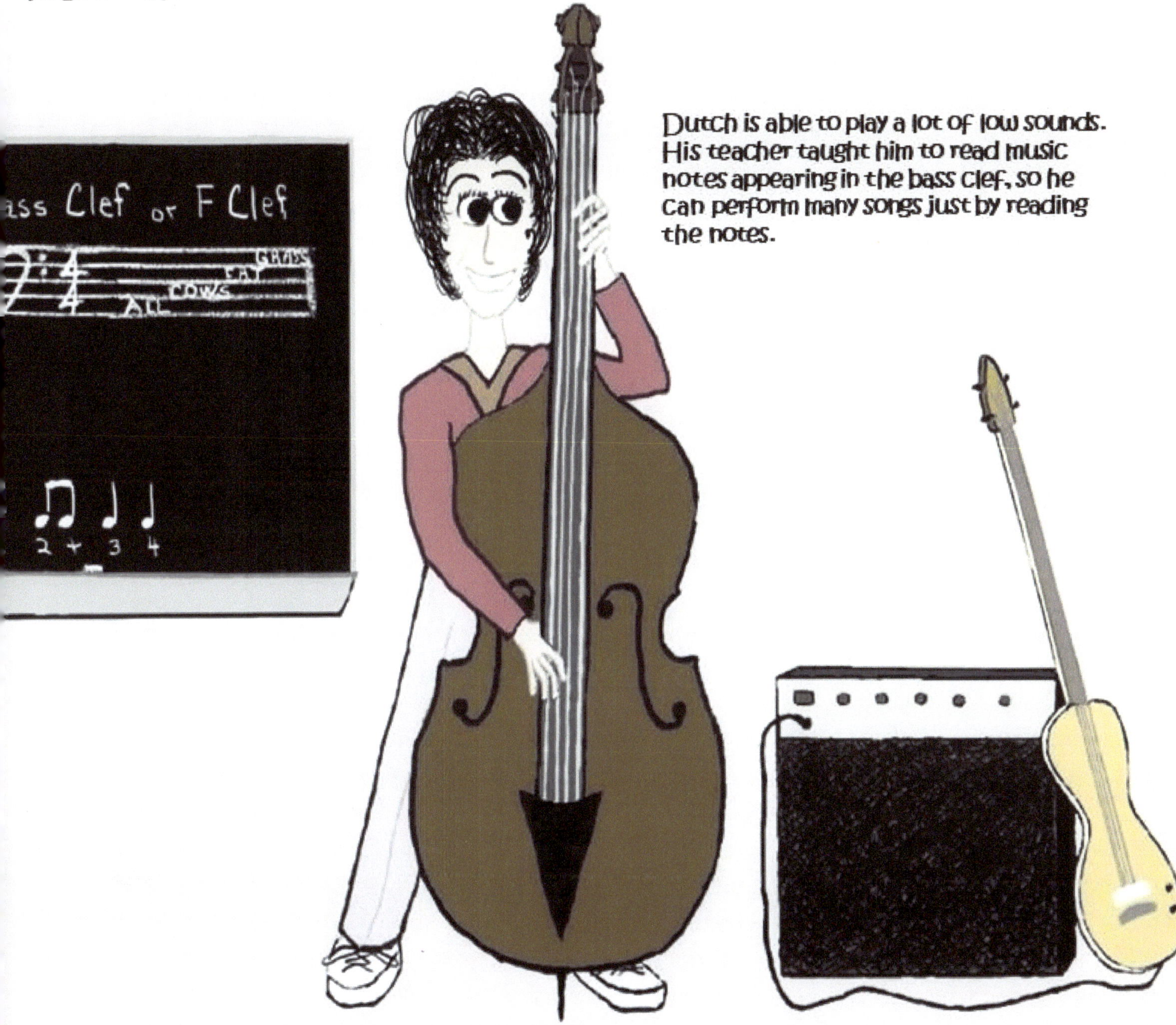

Dutch is able to play a lot of low sounds. His teacher taught him to read music notes appearing in the bass clef, so he can perform many songs just by reading the notes.

Qwater plays both the acoustic and electric guitar. He loves to twang, bend, swipe, slide, and scratch upon his six-string guitar. Each string is tuned to a certain sound. Qwater recently moved to Realla from New Orleans and brought with him a love of zydeco, jazz, blues, ragtime, and opera.

Eighty-Eight tickles the ebonies and ivories with great skill and passion. The keyboard often makes giggles and funny sounds when he pushes its buttons. He uses all of his fingers, including the pinky and the thumb, to play. He plays two or more notes at the same time, or what his teachers like to call "chords." Eighty-Eight enjoys reggae and ska as well as African pop.

Suite Sixteen is the lead singer and the youngest of the Notable Characters. The voice is the most important instrument because we all have a voice that helps us express who we are and how we feel—for free! Even when we can't talk, we can write and express our inner voice.

Suite Sixteen loves to sing into the microphone, one sound or pitch after another, or what her parents like to call, "melody." Yes, she sings a sweet melody, that Suite Sixteen. She jumps and wiggles to the rhythm of Wholesome's foot on the drum set bass pedal.

She sings with great joy and energy, bouncing her bang about as she falls into a scat or a dance or both!

She loves Bossa Nova and Brazilian rhythms. Her favorite song to sing? "The Girl from Oompahnoomah."

The five Notable Characters all live next door to each other on Tone Row. Across the street is Poplar Park where every midday break from school they like to cart their instruments to the amphitheater stage, set up, and play for whoever is there to enjoy their music. There is form to their lives, shaped by the routine of learning and playing.

Once they arrive home from the nearby school, each Notable takes a nippy nap. Then, one by one, they emerge from the sleep-world to the waking-world and to the aroma of patties, coco bread, and the comforting scent of fresh linen hanging outside their windows. Now, they are really ready to start the development portion of their day.

Each Notable owns a cart, usually stored underneath the front porch steps. In these carts, they place their instruments and sound equipment. They will meet at Wholesome's gate to form a convoy of carts ready to be pulled into Poplar Park.

The Notable Characters are careful not to confuse their cart of instruments with the cart of toys in their bedrooms. There is a big difference between a toy and an instrument! When they arrive at the curb, they wait patiently for the flashing green symbol for crossing. Symbols are used all the time in life and in music!

Once in the park, the Notable Characters set up their equipment. They are mindful of the time they have before they have to return to school. The Notables have amassed quite a following of dragonflies, mongoose, ducks, dogs, cats, insects and outsects, students, vendors, and Metronoma workers. Indeed, over the course of the school year they have won the adoration of the entire community. One afternoon, they begin their theme song, "We Had Our Nap We Had Our Meal and Now We Feel Okay." Their infectious rhythms, chords, and melodies inspire delightful dancing, twists, turns, hops, stomps, stretches, and fluttering wings, which makes the sky grow even brighter with glorious sun. The tropical breezes settle butterflies down into the front row of wildflowers.

The song comes to its end and the crowd claps and flaps joyously. Suite Sixteen feels exhilarated and, though out of breath, manages to say, "Thank you, our next song will be 'Noise Will Be Noise.'"

Wholesome begins the count of the steady beat by clicking his drumsticks with a "One, two, three, four!" On the downbeat of the steady beat, the Notables sound the first chord. Suddenly the volume drops so low that only the butterflies lounging on the wildflower petals in the front row can hear.

Wholesome scans the sound equipment looking for a loose wire, until he sees a dangling plug held by the hand of his schoolyard rival—Wholelotta Rest!

Wholelotta is the eldest of the Rest siblings. She's their fearless leader and the loudest and most threatening to sound in general. Wholelotta feels that Rests are best. Agreeing with her are all the Rests: Halfheart Rest, Arma Rest, Footsy Rest, and their quarrelsome little first-grade brother, Un Rest.

The Rests are of the same age range as the Notables, but they attend a different school. The Rests have also formed a music group, however they don't have the admiration of the community like the Notable Characters do. Some argue that this is because the Rests lack sound while the Notables love to play and share beautiful music. The Rests are jealous of the Notable's success and Poplar popularity.

Eighty-Eight is ticked-off by the unexpected unplugging. "What'd you do dat ting for man? We clearly loved in de park man, yah man!"

"Where yaw git the gumption to unplug us? Yaw take de roux out the gumbo," Qwater says.

The crowd promptly begins booing the Rests as the realization of what just happened spreads from person to person.

Un Rest begins stomping on the stage yelling, "I *hate* that song because there aren't enough ... time outs!"

"He means breaks, where the sound stops for one count," adds Footsy Rest.

"Or eighth rests, you know, like one half of a *beat down*," says Arma Rest menacingly.
"Or *half* of a measure," says Halfheart Rest with a sigh.
Wholelotta bellows out, "This stage is *our* territory, so stay off of it!! The people want to hear our medley of *silence*, not 'Noise will Be Noise!'"

Dutch responds with, "Anything beats a zero, and that's what the five of you Rests add up to, a big fat zero... especially you WhOOOllotta!! If you like rests so much, go take a nap in the dirt and leave us alone."

Wholesome stares intently at Wholelotta. "Now plug us back in so we can continue our set."

"Don't worry guys, I'll plug us up," says Suite Sixteen to the rescue. She then cartwheels toward Wholelotta Rest and quickly snatches the cord from her hand before she can react. Suite Sixteen is very quick and nimble. She can speed read, run fast, and bebop scat, but she is careful to chew her food slowly.

By now, the Rests realize that the crowd didn't take to their interruption one bit, so they high tail it out of Poplar Park, dragging Un by his ear before he can do any more damage to the sound equipment. The mongoose become agitated, running amuck and pelting the Rests with pebbles as they flee toward Unpoplar Park way on the other side of Metronoma.

Wholesome doesn't think it's fair to throw pebbles at the Rests (Wholesome always tries to be fair), so he orders the mongoose to drop the pebbles and they do. Then he clicks his sticks four times and the Notables thrill the park patrons with sensational music once again.

The Rests are the only band at their school and they are eager to compete against the Notables.

Wholelotta is the soulful lead singer. She has a "whole lotta" attitude.

Arma Rest plays a miniature upright bass.

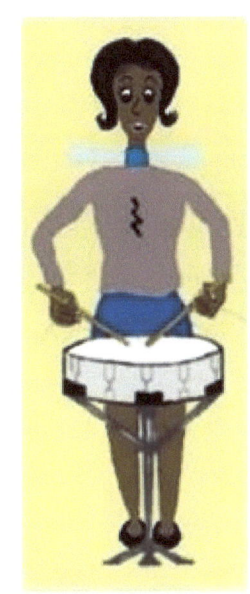

For all her love of shoes, Footsy loses them to play the drums in order to work the pedals with her bare feet and get a good grip on a steady beat.

Halfheart strums her guitar with a lackadaisical fall of the arm and swipe of the strings, concluding with a flippant upward motion. Her guitar looks like a strawberry with six strings stretching across it onto the neck, which doubles as a rain stick. She often drops her strawberry-shaped guitar picks.

Un plays the soothing harp, with a pluck here and a pluck there on randomly chosen strings. He loves his harp and carts it around like an ant hoisting a cornbread crumb above its head, not that he's extra strong, it's mostly adrenaline.

Back at school after their midday break, the Notables sense excitement in the air. Their teacher, Ms. Howard, is at the chalkboard hidden in a cloud of chalk dust. She is furiously writing information about the first annual battle of Realla's elementary school bands. A famous calypso singer named Diamond Duds is coming to help judge the event, which will be held in the school gym. Diamond Duds is Ms. Howard's favorite singer, so she hopes her group of talented kids will sign up to participate.

Qwater and Dutch sit in class waiting for the dust to settle. When they read the board, they get the bright idea to sign the Notables up for the event. They look at each other and nod in agreement.

The Realla Elementary Battle of the Bands Contest allows the best band from each of the island's five elementary schools to compete for a block of free studio recording time at Realla's top recording studio. This is the grand prize. Second-place winners will receive a $500.00 gift certificate redeemable at Mezzo Music Store, which sells instruments, accessories, and sheet music. Third-place winners will receive three free music lessons, provided by the teachers at Realla Conservatory of Music. Fourth- and fifth-place winners will be treated to a free kids meal at Soul Shine Seafood Eatery.

The other contestants are the Yuca Tones from Palm Elementary, Melody Mania from Charles Leo Elementary, and the Bratatatats from Seashore Academy.

There are five judges, two of whom flew into Realla for this special event and photo op. Of course, there's Ms. Howard's favorite entertainer, calypso singer Diamond Duds. Diamond wears sunglasses with diamonds encrusted in the frames. He smiles, laughs often, and breaks into a lyric he's been working on. Regional rap icon Blane Bling is also one of the judges. Then, there's the sophisticated mayor's wife, Ms. Ochorios; the owner of Soul Shine Seafood Eatery, Ms. Sparkle; and the superintendent of Realla's public school system, Mr. Missit.

All the bands compete fiercely, but the Notable Characters and the Rests deliver the most rousing performances, beating out the other contestants by a mile. Now, the battle comes down to just the two bands. The judges decide that the Rests should lead off the final round.

The Rests huddle together in a circle. Un asks, "What song can win this thing?" "How about that JB song, 'Get in Your Good Shoe?'" Footsy replies. Un is puzzled and asks, "Who's JB?" Halfheart half-jokingly suggests, "How about 'Rest On Your Laurels?'" Arma grows heated under her hot helmet and interjects, "Will you guys get serious?! Now's our chance to beat those ... those Notable Characters!" Wholelotta has the final say. "We'll do the song featuring Un, 'Doing the Rest Stop!'" "Yippee!" shouts Un, jumping up and down. "Can I do the dance too?" "You better!" Arma says. With a "Break!" and a clap, the Rests break away from their huddle to face the judges.

Blane Bling calls out, "Rests ... are you reaaaadddddeeehhhh? What's the name of your next song?"

The mayor's wife leans over to the superintendent, Mr. Missit, and whispers, "You know those Rests are good, but they stop a lot. What do you think?" "Look-a-here Ms. uuuhhh...First Lady, anytime those kids want to stop that racket, well that scores points with me," Mister Missit replies. They have a hearty chuckle. Wholelotta responds to Blane Bling, "We decided to perform our dance number, featuring me on vocals and our little brother Un 'Doing the Rests Stop!"
Ms. Sparkle of Soul Shine Seafood Eatery asks, "So what's the name of the song baby?" Wholelotta again says, "It's Un 'Doing the Rest Stop!" Diamond Duds, thinking Wholelotta was explaining the type of dance Un would do says, "Well, little girl, we know the boy wants to dance, but what's the name of the song?"

Arma, quite agitated, shouts, "It's called 'Doing the Rest Stop! Got it? Got it? Got it. KEEP IT!!!"

"Do we allow kids to wear helmets in school?" Mr. Missit asks Ms. Howard. She just shrugs her shoulders, too distracted by Diamond Duds' sparkling frames to pay much attention to the contest.

Meanwhile, Un's coda-symbol-shaped eyes spin in their sockets as his excitement to finally get from behind the harp and shake a leg grows. Footsy does the count off and the Rests go into "Doing the Rest Stop," a funky dance number.

Just when the audience catches onto Un's dance moves, the song freezes. There is a smattering of applause mixed with a smattering of confusion.

A moment later, the Rests begin again. Wholelotta gives her all. She kicks off her shoes and rolls around the gym, coming close to Wholesome, then moving away, yelling "ouch" when she rolls over Footsy's shoe. But, the crowd responds to the "ouch" favorably, shouting "Sing that song girl!"

Then, once again, the music stops.

The Rests just cannot help themselves from stopping. Diamond Duds shakes his head in disappointment. The superintendent calls out, "Bravo!" Blane Bling, not really noticing the music's stops and starts, jumps up on the judges' table next to his stack of CDs, throws his hands in the air, and waves them like he just doesn't care. He is offbeat, but doesn't seem to mind because he's having too much fun.

Qwater turns to the Notables and says, "You know what yaw, that music sounds an awful lot like a song I heard back home."

Just then, five Mongoose creep toward the stage. The next time the Rests stop, a curious thing happens. To everyone's surprise, the mongoose scramble onstage, grab the musical equipment that had been set up for the Notables, and start playing the instruments, or at least trying to. The Rests don't take too kindly to this, especially Arma, remembering the pelting they took in Poplar Park.

The Rests continue to play, knowing that the show must go on. Un keeps on dancing, oblivious to the commotion, but Halfheart desperately tries to shoo the mongoose off stage. When her attempts fail, she starts to cry, dropping her strawberry-shaped pick to the floor.

Seeing this, Qwater feels sorry for her. His empathy spreads from Notable to Notable and from judge to judge. Finally, Wholesome bellows out, "Hey, that's our stuff! Get off the stage!" But this time (unlike in Poplar Park) the mongoose don't listen to Wholesome, even going so far as to switch instruments and juggle his drumsticks. The audience erupts in laughter.

Suite Sixteen, who'd been taking a quick study of the situation, comes up with a bright idea.

"Don't worry guys, I know how to get those feisty mongoose off the stage. Just let me grab my trampoline from the storage room. They love to jump!"

She darts away to get her trampoline. When she returns, she positions the trampoline in front of the stage and starts jumping on it, bang-a-bouncing. Sure enough, those giggling mongoose leap onto the trampoline one after another and go giggling out the window.

The Rests smile at the Notables for the first time ever! They are grateful and decide to invite the Notables onstage to join them. Both bands begin the song, "Doing the Rest Stop."

This time, instead of the mongoose causing a ruckus, the Notables add melody. The Notables keep playing when the Rests stop and when the Notables stop, the Rests keep playing... and they make beautiful music together.

Un grabs Suite Sixteen by the hand and they do the "Rest Stop." Quater's guitar completes Halfheart's efforts, with his swipes and swings. Wholesome's third eye twinkles and rolls around in his head as Wholelotta shimmies and shakes all over the gym floor. Eighty-Eight pounds the keys, much to Arma's delight. Dutch's bass playing really complements Footsy's footwork on the bass drum pedal.

And when the song ends, the crowd goes wild. The judges take no time in agreeing that both bands should get the grand prize. So, the Notable Characters and the Rests would get the free recording studio time. In the near future, the two bands can look forward to competing on the charts! As for now, they congratulate each other.

Wholesome clicks his sticks four times and the Notable Characters in harmony with the Rests, begin "We Had Our Nap We Had Our Meal And Now We Feel Okay!"

About the Author

Leonard B. Rountree received his B. M. Composition degree from Howard University. He is a recording artist, musician, and educator, born in Washington. D. C. and raised in Maryland. He has Also written a musical based on "The Notable Characters" called "Swirl." A Few of the songs mentioned in this book appear as tracks on his album "Gainful Enjoyment."

Washentertainment
Washen Publishing
Artrac records
For inquiries write to:
Washentertainment
P. O. Box 324
Hyattsville, MD 20781-0324
Visit Washentree.com

www.ingramcontent.com/pod-product-compliance
Lightning Source LLC
LaVergne TN
LVHW071028070426
835507LV00002B/72